Wrestle and Fight and Pray

THOUGHTS ON
CHRISTIANITY AND CONFLICT

John L Bell

Series Editor: *Duncan B Forrester*

SAINT ANDREW PRESS

EDINBURGH

First published in 1993 by
SAINT ANDREW PRESS
121 George Street, Edinburgh EH2 4YN

ISBN 0 7152 0681 8

British Library Cataloguing in Publication Data
A catalogue record for this book
is available from the British Library.

ISBN 0715206818

Cover photograph by *Paul Turner.*

Cover design by *Mark Blackadder.*

Printed and bound by Bell and Bain Ltd, Glasgow.

WRESTLE and FIGHT and PRAY

Contents

Editor's Introduction

ALL down the ages Christians have reflected on their faith and its bearing on life. These reflections have taken a great variety of forms, but one of the most common has been the sermon. For generations notable preachers were well-known public figures, and books of sermons were a well-known literary genre. In many places people queued to hear great preachers, whose sermons were reported in the press, and discussed and dissected afterwards. Sermons launched great movements of mission, and revival, and social change. Sometimes influential preachers were imprisoned by the authorities so that their disturbing challenge should not be heard.

Nowhere was this tradition more lively than in Scotland. But today, some people say, the glory has departed. If you want to find great preaching today, the critics say, go to Africa, or Latin America, or to Black churches in the States. No longer in Scotland do people pack in their hundreds into huge churches to hear great preachers. The sermon seems to have lost its centrality in Scottish life. The conviction and the emotional surcharge that once sustained a great succession of notable preachers seems hard to find today. Has secularisation destroyed the appetite for sermons? Has the modern questioning of authority eroded the preaching office? Do Christians no longer reflect on their faith, or do they do it in other and newer ways?

This series of books shows that the tradition of preaching is still very much alive and well. It has changed, it is true, and it has adapted to new circumstances and new challenges. It is not the same as it was in the long afterglow of the Victorian pulpit. Reflection by the Scots on their faith, as these books illustrate, is perhaps more varied than it was in the past, and their sermons are briefer. But Scottish preaching is still passionate, thoughtful, biblical, challenging, and deeply concerned with the relevance of the gospel to the needs of today's world.

The reflections on the Christian faith in these books are challenging, disturbing, nourishing. They proclaim a Word that is alive and active, and penetrates to the depths of things, a Word that speaks of hope and worth, of forgiveness and new beginnings, of justice, peace and love. And so they invite the reader to engage afresh with the everlasting gospel.

Duncan B Forrester

Acknowledgments

I WISH to express my gratitude to Duncan Forrester who first approached and encouraged me to prepare this material for publication; to Margaret Simpson, my secretary, who laboured to make sense of manuscripts which had never been intended for publication; and to the congregations to whom I first preached these words, without whose listening the preaching would have been in vain.

John L Bell
APRIL 1993

Dedicated to the Memory
of my Mentors—
Robert Allan
and
Colin R M Bell
who preached and believed

1

Changeless and Changing

Readings: Hosea 2:14-23; John 15:1-17

Most people like love stories.
Sales of Mills and Boon novels confirm it,
as do long queues outside cinemas whenever a new celluloid
romance is released.

Whether it's in print or on film,
most love stories fall into one of two categories.

The first category we might call LOVE AGAINST THE ODDS.
… this is the Romeo and Juliet variety.
It's even the Cinderella variety.

Such stories tell how two lovers struggle to maintain and deepen
their relationship in the face of opposition. In the case of Romeo
and Juliet, the opposition comes from their warring families. In
the case of Cinderella, the opposition comes from two ugly sisters
with hairy chests and whiskers on their chins.

And when people read of, or see, this kind of tale, they come
away with their hearts warmed when love triumphs.

The second type of love story we might call LOVE IN THE FACE
OF DISLOYALTY.

… this is the kind of story which is as much witnessed in the daily papers as in novels and films.

It's the kind of story in which one partner in a relationship—often the woman—retains her devotion to her husband or lover
> despite his reckless living,
> despite his chasing after other women,
> despite his obsession with personal ambition,
> despite his treatment of her as a utensil.

Despite all this, the woman remains faithful,
her love forgives and constantly reconciles.

Of course, we don't have to go to the extremes of popular journalism to find evidence of this sort of love story.

I'm frequently annoyed when I'm in company where a man is receiving a presentation from his firm or club or even his church.

He'll be extolled to the heavens for his ardour and virtue,
presented with a trophy,
and then the male who is making the speeches will say, rather condescendingly,
'Of course, behind every good man there is a good woman',
and offer the customary bouquet to the wife.

And what is sometimes flagrantly overlooked in that situation is that while *he* was chasing ambition,
> while *he* was downing the shorts at the nineteenth hole
> courtesy of the company's expense account,
> while *he* was making the decisions and taking the floor,
> while *he* was forgetting her,

she was remembering him … and his children
and his stomach
and all his other needs.

There's one of these stories of LOVE IN THE FACE OF DIS-LOYALTY in the Bible … though it's not about an unfaithful, ambitious and cavalier husband.

It's about a wife who goes whoring behind her husband's back and sometimes in front of his face.

And though the husband feels like leaving her,
though the husband at times would gladly abandon her to discover the shallow affections of her playboys and toyboys;
though the husband sometimes wants to call her the foulest names in his vocabulary;
he doesn't do any of these things.

Instead he decides to be more faithful, more loving, more loyal, and he says to his wife, in all her wantonness:

'I'll keep my promise to make you mine.
I'll keep you mine forever.'

And people like you and me, reading this tale, might feel that the man is going too far, that he is showing compassion well beyond the call of duty and reasonableness.

People like you and me, if we met this husband in the street and had a quiet word with him, would maybe suggest that he separate, advise him to divorce, start again with a worthier wife.

3

But we dare not.

Because this faithful husband is God.
And the shameless hussy of a wife is us.

*   *   *

The prophecy of Hosea offers a penetrating insight into the inability of the people of God to keep their word, to be loyal. The people of God are depicted as the ones who go for easy relationships, who forget what they have promised, who distance themselves from their Maker.

But the prophecy of Hosea also offers a penetrating insight into the heart of God …
   whose faithfulness does not depend on us playing fair,
   whose loyalty does not depend on us keeping our word,
   whose devotion does not depend on our love always
      being at full strength.

God is faithful, always faithful
because God is God
and can be nothing else.

And it is one of the unspeakable privileges of anybody who preaches the Gospel to declare this: that God's love is changeless. You cannot stop God loving you. God has made a promise to you and it was sealed at your baptism that he would never leave you or forsake you.

And just because sometimes you forget him;
      just because sometimes you put your personal ambition on a

4

higher plain than your faith;
just because sometimes you don't feel that your relationship
with your creator is at full strength;
just because sometimes you can't stand the Church;
don't think that God feels the same way about you.
Don't judge God by your standards!

God is faithful
even when you have no thought for him.

God cannot be other,
because in his love and mercy, God is changeless.

And what a glorious thing to realise,
either if you're unsure about the strength of your own commitment
of if you have suffered at the expense of someone else's fidelity.

God is love
and that love is constant and changeless.

* * *

But when I say that God is changeless,
I realise that I say not only a very comforting thing,
but a very dangerous thing.

Because it only takes a little thought or a little thoughtlessness
to deduce that we should be changeless too.

If from Scripture we learn that we are made in God's image, and
we learn that God is changeless, we presume that we should be
changeless too.

But it doesn't work that way.

The proof that we have been grasped by the changeless love of God is that we never remain the same,
but are transformed, converted, turned upside down, inside out.

Some years ago, a boy called Jonathan used to come about our house. He was invariably untidy, a bit slovenly and often incomprehensible. He slurred his speech badly.

He disappeared to England for a couple of years and returned on our doorstep late one Friday night. He looked different and he sounded different, but I didn't get a chance to ask much because it was late and besides he wanted a bath ... something he had never requested before.

So I ran the bath for him and when I returned to show him where the towels were kept, I noticed what looked like coloured plastic baubles, about half a dozen of them, in the bathwater. And as I looked, they melted and their colour and scent began to spread.

I wondered if perhaps Jonathan had an allergy or a skin infection and whether these were for medicinal purposes. But he assured me they were not for illness, but for pleasure. Bath oils, he informed me, were the 'in thing'.

As he spent the next day with us, a whole lot of changes began to emerge—not just in his speech and his appearance, but in his attitude to life, in his ability to save money, in his confidence in a crowd. But why?

Eventually the truth came out and the penny dropped.

He had met a girl who loved him.
Oh, he had known other girls in his life,
but they had made no impression.
This girl, however, quite definitely loved him,
and because he knew and felt and believed that he was loved,
all things changed.

People who know that they are loved,
and people who accept the love of another, are transformed.
People who do not change,
who are not touched or influenced or moved by another,
have a shallowness in their relationship

And this is true of the relationship of the people of God to their
Maker.

Go from the beginning of the Bible to the end and see if you
encounter anyone who has met God and stayed the same.

Some people ... like Sarah and Hannah and Elizabeth and Mary
became fertile and gave birth to children.
Some people ... like Moses and Abraham and Jonah
went on a journey.
Some people ... like David and Isaiah and Paul
wrote love songs.
Some people ... like Jeremiah and Matthew and Zacchaeus
got rid of their money and changed their
lifestyle.
Some people ... like Peter and Andrew and James and John
changed their jobs.
Some people ... like the host of cripples and blind folk and lepers
whose names we'll never know

changed from begging to dancing,
from sitting on the circumference
to being in the centre.

And why? … why? …
Because the changeless love of God had had its effect on them.

And we … we, if we are all seized and fascinated by that love,
will never remain the same,
but CHANGE from glory into glory
till in heaven we take our place.

Stagnancy, immovability, is no virtue in a Christian.
It is a sign of spiritual lock-jaw, from which we should pray to be delivered.

* * *

But what is true of us as individuals is true of the Church also, the Bride of Christ.

Can you imagine what kind of a relationship a man and wife would have if, fifty years after their wedding, she was still wearing a veil and carrying the same bouquet as on her wedding day?

Can you imagine what kind of marriage they would have if, fifty years after the wedding, she was still saying the same things to him as she had said when they first met:

'I love your curly red hair
and your sparkling white teeth'

… even though he had become as bald as a coot,
   and wore dentures?

The Church as the Bride of Christ
has to change as she responds to the insights Scripture offers
and the love which God shares.
We are the Body of Christ, not his corpse;
and if there are no signs of growth, change and development
then we should call for the undertaker rather than the evangelist.

There's a story told about two elderly ladies from Kelvinside who
decided to go on an expedition to the far east.

So they came to Edinburgh and stayed in the North British Hotel
and despite all their expectations to the contrary, they enjoyed
themselves thoroughly.

When they got home, they couldn't stop talking about the great
time they had had.

One day their cousin Agnes came to visit.

Effie, the older sister, started on about the wonders of
Edinburgh ....

   'And you should have seen where we were living, Agnes,'
   she said,
   'We were in the North British Hotel,
   We had a lovely room with a lovely view,
   and best of all a beautiful bathroom. Isn't that right, Nell?'

   Nell agreed,

'Do you know Agnes, it was tiled from ceiling to floor.
It had a heated towel rail,
gold taps on the sink,
and the biggest bath you've ever seen.

'It's such a pity we couldn't use it.
We only stayed until Wednesday—
Thursday's our bath night.'

Of course, we laugh at that kind of inflexibility;
but it's a pattern of behaviour into which the Church is ever in
danger of falling.

It is in the Church that people, irrespective if their background,
their politics, their life experience, are at their most conservative.

So … despite eighty per cent of our congregation being female,
we pray that all *men* might be saved
and sing 'name him *brothers* name him.'

So … despite the fact that in Africa and South America, the
Church is growing, while in Britain it decreases in strength,
we still think that we should be sending missionaries,
rather than receiving them.

So … in churches where there are fifty attenders
and five hundred seats,
we sit apart as if the body of Christ had acne rather than
unity.

And, if anyone should breathe the word 'change', the grumble
and rumour goes around about 'change for change's sake'.

If the doctor said to us,
    'I'm changing your prescription …
    I feel these tablets would be better for you',
Would we say 'change for change's sake'?

If the car mechanic said,
    'I want to change your brake blocks … these new ones are
     better suited to your car',
Would we say 'change for change's sake'?

Then should we say it to God,
    especially when with God it is *never*, NEVER,
    change for change's sake;
It is *always*, ALWAYS, change for love's sake.

In St John's Gospel,
Jesus talks about himself as being the vine and we the branches.

And the picture he gives is slightly painful, because he does not
say we can ramble where we want or remain the same.

He says that if we are united to him,
we will be pruned,
        cut back,
        altered,
        changed … to become more fruitful still.

If we know we are loved by God
we will not be scared by that kind of transformation,
We will embrace it,
knowing that it is God's will
to make all things new.

2

When these Things
begin to happen

Readings: Isaiah 52:7-10; Luke 21:23-33

Text: Luke 21:28

> *When these things begin to happen, stand up and raise your heads because your Salvation is near.*

I was looking forward to today,
not particularly because I was preaching in Edinburgh. I would have looked forward just as much had I been in Foula or Tiree.

I was looking forward to today because this is *Advent Sunday*.

The Church, thank God, does not wait until the change of the calendar to celebrate a new beginning. Four weeks before Christmas comes the Sunday on which the prophecies are again read about how God promised to send a Messiah. And like any family looking forward to the birth of a new child, the Holy Catholic Church begins to prepare for the Nativity.

I was looking forward to today for a long time.

Because, for me, this year has been a very hard year, and not just in terms of work (though it's been a tough year for that), but more in terms of the toll it has taken on people.

During the year two of my oldest friends died
and so did two of my youngest, both in their twenties.
It's been a hard year in terms of people becoming ill,
not with sicknesses which have a predictable recovery
period
but with nervous breakdown,
exhaustion,
depression,
and, compounding all these, M.E.

It's been a hard year learning also of those whose sickness has no cure.

It's been a hard year seeing families in which I had presumed there was a steady depth of love, break up or exhibit that kind of marital strain which does not omen well for the future.

It's been a hard year at the door,
for though I do not live in the poorest part of Glasgow,
there seems to have been a never-ending stream of people coming up the path asking not for money but for food for themselves and their children.

So I was looking forward to today,
to Advent Sunday,
to hear God putting good news on the agenda again,
to sing O COME, O COME IMMANUEL
to this heart
and to that home;
and to this person
and to that predicament.
O COME, O COME IMMANUEL!

I *was* looking forward
until I discovered the reading for today.

Having resolved this year to follow the lectionary, I looked up
the appointed readings for Advent Sunday.

THE OLD TESTAMENT:

Isaiah: 'How beautiful upon the mountains are the
feet of those who bring good news'
… lovely words, the more evocative because
I've known them since childhood as set to
music by Handel in the Messiah.

THE EPISTLE:

1 *Thessalonians*: … perhaps not so well known as Isaiah, but
having in it the image of the kingdom coming
like a thief in the night.

So far so good.

THE
GOSPEL

Luke 21:25-33: 'THERE WILL BE STRANGE THINGS
HAPPENING TO THE SUN, THE MOON
AND THE STARS.
ON EARTH WHOLE COUNTRIES WILL
BE IN DESPAIR,
AFRAID OF THE ROAR OF THE SEA AND
THE RAGING TIDES.

'PEOPLE WILL FAINT WITH FEAR AS
THEY WAIT FOR WHAT IS COMING

OVER THE WHOLE EARTH,
AND THE POWERS IN SPACE WILL BE
DRIVEN FROM THEIR COURSES.'

Enough! Enough!

Enough for two reasons.

* * *

First, this is the kind of language in the Scriptures which I find hard to handle and which, most of the time, I avoid.

It's not a parable; it's not a miracle; it's not the story of an encounter; it's not even a wise saying of Jesus. It's part of what is known as APOCALYPTIC LITERATURE.

It's to do with the end of time, with the day of judgement, with the final state of the world, with catastrophes which will indicate that the end is near. It's the nearest thing to religious science fiction.

There's not a lot of it in the Bible. It is most evident in the books of Daniel and Revelation, but the Gospels also have some of it.

It is writing which is both too vague and too specific. It leaves itself open to interpretation in a thousand ways and some people act as if it were the only biblical writing which was important.

There are always apocalypse addicts around somewhere: sometimes very young Christians … sometimes long in the tooth.

They become caught up with trying to interpret the day and the hour and the means of earth's ultimate disaster. Obsessed by the number 666—the number of the Beast—they see it encoded in pop songs, or imagine it tattooed on the head of everyone from Fidel Castro to Pope John Paul II.

For years those people have identified the Soviet Union as the Scarlet Woman, the Evil Empire, the Beast in the Revelation of St John the Divine. But now, in the light of *perestroika* and *glasnost* they have had to re-orientate their insights.

This, of course, is no new thing. Apocalypse addicts have been around for a long time. In AD 999, convinced that the end was going to come at the termination of the millennium, they encouraged people to get up on to the hills and mountains on Hogmanay to meet the coming Saviour.

The Jehovah's Witnesses are perhaps the most consistent of this religious sub-culture. I remember reading an account of a town council meeting in Kilmarnock in 1968. A discussion had arisen over the request of the local Jehovah Witness group to take a ten year lease out on a piece of council property.

One of the Councillors stood up and said, 'I'm very surprised to hear they want a ten year lease. Last week they were at my door assuring me the world was going to end in three.'

Serious students of this type of literature fall into three camps:

Those who say apocalyptic writing is highly prophetic and if only we could crack the code, we would understand it;
those who say that the apocalyptic writing was only applicable to biblical times and many of the prophecies have already come true;

and those—like Alan Boesak of South Africa, and a great many other people living in similar situations of social injustice—who say that these passages of Scripture only become intelligible at certain times and in certain places. They may be relevant at one time in one place, but not necessarily at the same time in another.

*   *   *

And that may be the second reason why I wanted to say 'Enough! Enough!' when reading the passage in Luke's Gospel.

These words reverberate,
> bristle,
> resonate with significance in the face of what this past year has brought us.

'THERE WILL BE STRANGE THINGS HAPPENING TO THE SUN, THE MOON AND THE STARS.'
... and if we allow them to represent the supra-terrestrial realms:
> the air, the atmosphere, the stratosphere,
> the ecosphere,
then strange things *have* happened.

For the sun, presumed since creation to be the friend of the earth, has in recent years been identified as the enemy: not because it has done anything wrong, but because the depletion, the dent, the damage in the ozone layer has weakened our defences against its harmful rays. And though damage, caused by men and women, governments and industry, is not irreversible, there are plenty of words, but minimal action to repair what has gone wrong.

'ON EARTH WHOLE COUNTRIES WILL BE IN DESPAIR,

AFRAID OF THE ROAR OF THE SEAS AND THE RAGING TIDES.'
… Amen, say people as far apart as Bangladesh and Bournemouth. For the process of global warming threatens to melt the polar ice caps and raise the level of the sea, such that our natural defences will be insufficient. And at the same time, of course, the unbridled pollution of the ocean ensures that its produce and its water are to be looked upon with suspicion.

'PEOPLE WILL FAINT FOR FEAR AS THEY WAIT FOR WHAT IS COMING OVER THE WHOLE EARTH.'
… and don't these words reverberate in a thousand caverns of the contemporary conscience?

We have recently had highlighted just one of the threats that make people faint and fear at what is coming over the earth. WORLD AIDS DAY (not national Aids Day, but *international*) highlights how Aids is no longer a health hazard prevalent among male homosexuals, but a phenomenon which is now spreading as an epidemic throughout the heterosexual world, threatening to decimate the populations of countries such as Uganda, and most miserably being represented in the emaciated faces of Ceausescu's orphans in Romania.

Those who have a care for the world's health may well faint with fear at the future prospects.

But, in recent years, others may have fainted with fear at the outcome of the decision of the United Nations to permit the use of armed force in the Gulf crisis.

The destructive potential of that line of action should have had us all shaking in our shoes with fear and rage ...

Not just because Saddam Hussein is a brutal man whose gross-
ness was exhibited in the gassing of the Kurdish population in
his own country;

Nor just because hypocrisy reeks from every chimney in the UN
building—for when South Africa invaded Namibia and refused to
leave, or when Israel invaded the West Bank and refused to leave,
no such militaristic ultimatum was allowed.

Nor should we faint with fear and rage just because the policies
of the West are overwritten and underwritten with self-interest
masquerading as humanitarianism.

As a US Commander said recently,
'If the Kuwaitis were growing carrots, nobody would bother',
but because it is oil, oil which the West requires to keep the upper
hand in world affairs; because it's oil, all the high flown rhetoric
of justice and mortality is put on parade.

No ... more than that ... more than that!

The earth should shake with terror at the prospect
because this world in this era cannot afford another war.

The fifteen million refugees who wander the earth waiting to be
wanted cannot afford another war.

The debt ridden nations of the South
—Ghana, Indonesia, Argentina, Brazil—
these poorest of countries which send thirty billion dollars a year

to the North in interest payments from money loaned years ago cannot afford another war.

The 3.5 million peasant families in Peru for whom there has been no harvest,
and the countless million peasant families in Ethiopia and Eritrea for whom there will be no harvest,
cannot afford a war.

WHO WOULD BLAME GOD IF HE DAMNED US TO HELL FOR MOUNTING AN EXPENSIVE EXTERMINATION PROGRAMME IN THE MIDDLE EAST IN THE FACE OF THE KNOWN BUT AVOIDABLE HUNGER AND THIRST OF A QUARTER OF HUMANITY?

Yes, yes,
'People will faint from fear as they wait for what is coming over the earth.'

These words in all their terror and truth resonate today in our hearing.
This is our situation and it is horrible to contemplate.

So what does it mean and what are we to do?

… tie sandwich boards to each other and walk the streets advertising that the end is nigh and we should prepare to meet our Maker?

On this Advent Sunday, when these words of Jesus take on a relevance which they have not had for a long time, we are not left in despair, for listen:

'WHEN THESE THINGS BEGIN TO HAPPEN,
STAND UP AND RAISE YOUR HEADS,
BECAUSE YOUR SALVATION IS NEAR.'

The Word of God is *not* look around and get depressed at how
bad things are,
but look up because your salvation is near.

There may be some who would like to conjecture that the end
is near.
There may be some who might think that God is about to roll down
the final curtain.

If that is God's will and if that is God's judgement ... so be it.
But on Advent Sunday, we are not encouraged to speculate on
the wrath of the Almighty, but to celebrate the power of his love.

For God has already chosen to intervene in this messy world and
to do that not in terms of a celestial army,
nor in terms of a plague to wipe out the infidels and keep the
favoured folk alive,
nor in terms of a blue print guaranteed to avoid disaster.

God has promised to intervene in the form of a child to be born in
the Middle East ...
unwanted, suspected,
at risk,
vulnerable
and, to the hard of heart, easily disposable.

*   *   *

When so much today threatens human life,
when so much today degrades human life,
when so much today barters with human life as if men and women
were merely statistical fodder for computers, rather than the bear-
ers of the image of the Maker of heaven and earth,
when so much today is at risk—
we celebrate that God has chosen to take on human life,

> to invest it with a value it cannot find in itself,
> to initiate a process of salvation whereby even the
> most inveterate warmonger might be transformed if
> he or she but glanced at the nakedness of God's love,
> and the magnitude of his risk.

As this season unfolds,
as the precariousness of the earth becomes more evident,
we have an option.

We can either look around at the vulnerability of the world and
expect the Day of Judgement hoping that we will be spared.

Or we can stand up and raise our heads

> and gaze at the vulnerability of God who takes flesh
> first in the baby of Bethlehem
> and then also in every threatened child in Iraq
>> in every starving child in Ethiopia,
>> in every battered child in Britain,
>> in every orphaned child in Romania,

offering us the choice: hurt me
> or   love me.

3

The Hope you have in You

Readings: Genesis 19:15-26; 1 Peter 3:8-17

Text: 1 Peter 3:15

> *Be ready at all times to answer anyone who asks you to explain the hope you have in you.*

What do you make of the story, the one from the Old Testament, about Lot's wife turning into a pillar of salt?

Is it the kind of story which makes you rankle with embarrassment in case your children, or someone else's children, ask you if it's true?

Is it the kind of story which, if you had the opportunity, you might cut out of the Bible altogether, along with a couple of other dubious tales, like Sarah getting pregnant when she is ninety or Jonah being swallowed by a whale?

When you hear the story, do you wish that somebody would ask an eminent archaeologist to do a survey of all the rock structures within a five mile radius of Sodom and Gomorrah to establish definitively whether or not there is a column which in any way bears a resemblance to a middle-aged woman?

Or do you just put down the story as an example of how these ancient Jews had vivid imaginations and a good way with words?

Jesus doesn't allow us, however much we might want to, to be so quickly dismissive.

Because to him the story of Lot and his family was important— as was the story of Sarah and Abraham, as was the story of Jonah. Indeed in the middle of a speech in Luke's Gospel we find Jesus saying with some urgency to his listeners, 'Remember Lot's wife!'

For him, for the one we call our Lord, this ancient story had a value.

However bizarre it might seem,
however unlikely, it has been recorded for a purpose.

NOT … I suggest,

NOT … so that our minds might boggle,
but so that our spirits might be fed.

*　　*　　*

So, what of Lot's wife?
> What of this woman who was told to flee with her husband
> from a city about to be destroyed?

> What of this woman who looked back … and who was turned
> into a pillar of salt?

Let me move, for a minute, from the unfamiliar to the familiar.

I had a phone call the other night from a friend of whom I'm very fond. He's a retired minister. His name is George. I agree with him in most things, but one area of great disagreement is music.

I enjoy singing hymns. He can't stand singing, not just hymns but anything. I asked him one day why that was and he said,

> 'Because I'm tone deaf.
> I can't sing'

'Who told you that?' I asked.

> 'Do you really want to know?' he replied.

'Yes, tell me.'

> 'Okay, it was when I was in my second year at secondary school and I was put in the junior boys' choir. We had a big music teacher called Jake Johnson and in the middle of this song, he stopped and brought me out to the front and said to me, "See you son … in future just you mime".'

Then George went on,

> 'I can remember it as if it were yesterday. That's the day my singing stopped.'

Now, just as an experiment, I asked a group of twelve men how many of them were 'tone deaf' or couldn't sing. Four out of the twelve admitted to it. And when I asked them if they could put a picture to when they discovered that, everyone could.

Three said it was a teacher who had told them they were 'tone deaf' at a delicate stage in their adolescence. One said he went with a girl who told him to shut up when he started to sing along with the radio.

All of them could picture very clearly the event, the person, the time and place when this had happened; and every time they were asked to sing, they looked back to the day when their confidence was destroyed, and thus they are now incapable of doing anything but keeping dumb.

I'm glad to say that now four out of five of these men now sing regularly. Why? Because they stopped looking back at the moment when their confidence had been destroyed.

IS THAT A FAR CRY FROM LOT'S WIFE?

*   *   *

Let me mention two other sorts of people who suffer from a kind of paralysis.

I think of a family on the other side of the city who, a number of years ago, sustained the loss of their twelve year old son. He was knocked down and killed by a car.

He had been a very active boy, a very lively youngster and the family were decimated. For whatever reason—and I don't know the reason—they decided that they would leave their son's bedroom exactly the way it was on the day he died.

So the room remained with his toys on the floor, with his football scarves and pop posters on the wall ... something which they looked into every now and then.

And that family never began to cope with their grief realistically until they repainted the room and got rid of the things in it which were no longer useful, but which reminded them of a numbing tragedy.

IS THAT A FAR CRY FROM LOT'S WIFE?

*　　*　　*

Or let me mention a girl of nineteen, Jane, who had been molested by a friend of the family when she was seven. As a child she had tried to tell her parents this. They had gone off the head, called her filthy, said she was imagining things, and scarred her mind in such a way that every day throughout her childhood and adolescence, she was haunted by the memory of the way she had been abused.

Such was the effect that at the age of nineteen she was no more emotionally mature than she had been a decade previously and her self worth would have been rated at zero.

*　　*　　*

There is a pattern of human behaviour which this strange story of Lot's wife sets out in terms which are as true to life in the twentieth century AD as they were in the days of Lot and his family.

There is something in the destructive experiences of life which holds a morbid fascination. We know that when a building is on fire and crowds gather around to see the building disintegrate.

We know that when there is a disaster and the newspapers vie with each other to see who can get the most lurid pictures of the suffering victims.

We know it in the sales of horror videos which have no pretence of doing anything other than providing blood and gore to whet the viewer's thirst for another video which might be even bloodier or gorier.

The story of Lot's wife is about all people, even those from the best and safest families, when they become so fascinated by the destructive forces in life that they themselves end up part of the destruction.

I would venture to suggest that if this tale had been written in the age of the car, rather than the age of the donkey, it might have had a different ending. It might have read:

> *The Lord began the destruction of the cities of Sodom and Gomorrah. And behold the wife of Lot took to her car and sped away. But as she skirted the town on the motor way, the sound of the destruction and the glow of flames in the sky encouraged her to do that which had been forbidden her.*

> *So keeping her hands on the wheel, she looked back and became curiously fascinated by the sight of the destruction, so fascinated that she forgot the road ahead of her and drove her car over the parapet of a bridge.*

This is part of the human predicament, which you and I, in greater or lesser measure, will have recognised in ourselves or in other people.

It may not be that, like my ministerial friend, you have looked back to the day when you were told you were tone deaf and have never sung since.

It may not be that you have suffered a bereavement and kept the deceased's room so much like a shrine that you became nothing more than a shadow of yourself.

It may not be that in childhood you were molested or had some other experience which plagued your mind for years thereafter, not allowing you to mature or move on.

But it may be that you know people who, when a relationship ended, became so obsessed with the way it ended that they began to believe they could never have a relationship again, and so romance or love died or stood still.

Or it may be that you know someone who was made redundant and the shock was so big that all she ever thinks of is the moment when she was told she was no longer wanted on the pay roll. Her self confidence died at that time and she is convinced she can never work again—bitterness and sourness and anger have turned someone who used to smile into a creature who always frowns.

This temptation, this tendency, to look with morbid fascination on what has gone wrong, or what is going wrong, is part of human life and the story of Lot's wife shows us what happens when that tendency goes too far. We become so obsessed with what is destructive, that we become destroyed ourselves.

Maybe it was in some way to counteract that human weakness that Peter in his first letter counselled new Christians with the words:

'Always be ready to give an account of the hope that is in you.'

Writing to people who had probably every bit as much reason to despair about the social trends, or the state of the Church, or the frustration of life, he doesn't encourage them to make an accurate critique of what is wrong in their life.

He doesn't write to encourage their cynicism about the society round about them.

He doesn't write to say, 'Always be ready to give an account of how sinful the world is!'

He asks them to give an account of the HOPE that is in them.

Because that, after all, is the gift of Christians to the world—HOPE.

There are some who may want to claim that the world is a wicked place, and every century shows different depths to which human depravity can sink.

That may be true, but that is not the last word, nor is it the first word. For in the beginning God made everything that is and declared that it was good. And in the end God shall make all things new.

There are some who might want to claim that this life is a vale of tears and that some folk get a rougher deal than others.

And that is true, but that is not the last word nor is it the first.

For in the beginning God commanded that love should be the principle which guides human actions, and in the end God has promised to wipe away the tears from all faces.

There are some who might want to dolefully lament that beggars can't be choosers and that it's everyone to their own station and too bad if you are at the bottom.

But heaven forbid that such sourness should ever come from the lips of a Christian. What kind of gospel is that?

If our lips must say anything, then let them tell the truth as Mary told it: that the humble shall be exalted, the hungry shall be fed, and the mighty and ruthless shall be pulled down from their thrones. That represents the hope that is in us, and that is real hope.

When God in Jesus Christ revealed himself on earth, he didn't go up to those who were dumb and say, 'I'm sorry you can't make a sound!' He said, 'Your mouths were made for singing', and he opened their mouths.

He didn't go up to those who had been socially or sexually or spiritually assaulted and say, 'You're in a bad way … I feel sorry for you!' He took them by the hand and lifted them to their feet and set them on a new path entirely.

When he was confronted by the prospect of certain death and annihilation at the hands of the enemies, he didn't say, 'Well, it looks like the final curtain; it's been nice knowing you all!' He said, 'I will be put to death and in three days I will rise again!'

It is not easy to live out that kind of hope.
It is not easy to look into the eyes of an ugly sinner and believe that there might be an angel in his or her soul whom only love and forgiveness will liberate.

It is not easy to look at the mask of darkness which covers Northern Ireland and the Middle East and see beyond it to a day when Protestant and Catholic, Jew and Arab will live together in peace.

But if we don't proclaim and celebrate that hope which is announced in the Scriptures and made flesh in Jesus Christ ... who else is going to?

Who else is going to, in a world where cynicism and a jaundiced view of human nature can so easily pass for normal?

I was once in Birmingham at a rally at which the Archbishop Desmond Tutu was speaking. He was answering questions from the audience. And someone, who might well have been a plant from the ultra right who were out to subvert his pastoral visit to Birmingham, asked what people in Britain could do to help black South Africans.

Tutu replied that he thought people already knew the action they could take ... to do with sanctions ... to do with protests ... to do with boycotting ... these had already been spelled out. And then his voice rose and he said, 'But do you really want to know what is the most important thing you can do for us?

'Do you really want to know …?
I will tell you …
pray for us.'

Then he said, 'When I go to see Alan Boesak after bricks have been thrown through his window, almost injuring his children, I expect to meet an angry and bitter man.

'When I go to see Frank Chicane after he has been told that if he doesn't shut up, his mother's life will be in danger, I expect to meet an angry and bitter man.

'When I go to see such people, I expect them to say, "We've had enough, Desmond … Let's take up arms … Let's stop being peacemakers".

'But instead I meet people who are patient and who are warm and who smile and who believe that a new heaven and earth are even now coming about, and why?

'Because your prayers help to keep alive the hope that is in them.'

4

Unless a Grain of Wheat shall fall

Readings: Philippians 2:6-11; John 12:20-32

Text: John 12:24

> *Unless a grain of wheat shall fall to the ground and die, it remains but a single grain with no life, but if it does die, it produces many grains.*

On Passion Sunday, as we look ahead, with Jesus, to the cross, we can ask with some appropriateness:
Why did Jesus die?

There is no other death in human history which is so renowned. The sign of the cross, wherever it appears, on a priest's alb or on a punk's earring, witnesses to the fact
>not just that Jesus died,
>
>nor just that Jesus died on a cross,
>
>but that *this death* has a significance no other deaths have ever had ... nor will ever have.

So, why did Jesus die?

In the face of libraries of books about the crucifixion,
>>the atonement,
>>the sacrificial offering,
>>the redemptive act;

in the face of all that has already been said or written, it is perhaps presumptuous to say anything more.

But it's maybe because so much has been written,
                because so much has been said,
that it may be helpful not to engage in some intense theological discourse, but to offer a few signposts.

*   *   *

Why did Jesus die?

The first signpost must read: THROUGH PHYSICAL CONSTRAINTS

And by that, I don't mean lack of breath
                or the consequence of severe bleeding.
I mean that there are some clearly discernible reasons as to why Jesus ended up on the cross, all to do with the fact that religious people didn't like him.

The crucifixion hadn't really much to do with the Romans.
Pilate, as Jesus pointed out, was just a pawn in the game.
Whether the Romans were cruel or kind is a secondary matter.
The fact was that only they, the occupying army, could arrange for public executions.
The Jews couldn't bump off whoever they liked. They had to convince the Romans that the person deserved to die.

Yet, in a way, the crucifixion didn't have much to do with the Jews.
Martha, Mary, Andrew, James, Magdalene were all Jews,
so were most of the folk Jesus healed, talked to, spent time with.

Peter's mother-in-law and blind Bartimaus were both Jews
and it would be preposterous to say that they were responsible
for Jesus ending up at Calvary.

It wasn't the Romans,
It wasn't the Jews … as a race …
It was religious people who engineered the crucifixion because
they didn't like Jesus.

And, in fairness to them, that was consistent throughout his life.
From his first sermon to his last public speech, the scribes and
the pharisees and the doctors of the law … the religious *power-brokers* were out to get him.

His words didn't suit them,
his appearance didn't please them,
his company didn't endear them,
and what he said about life
                    and faith
                    and God
was *anathema* to their ears.

'THIS MAN IS A FRIEND OF SINNERS'
'THIS MAN BREAKS OUR LAWS'
'THIS MAN DOES NOT RESPECT OUR TRADITIONS'
'THIS MAN UPSETS OUR CHURCH SERVICES'
(Oh yes, you find that at least ten times in the Gospels)
'THIS MAN TOUCHES PEOPLE WHO ARE DISEASED
                                OR DIRTY
                                OR DISGUSTING'
'THIS MAN ASSOCIATES WITH NON-BELIEVERS'

and worse
'THIS MAN CLAIMS THAT GOD APPROVES OF THIS TYPE
OF BEHAVIOUR'
and worse still
'THIS MAN ALLOWS PEOPLE TO CALL HIM GOD'S SON'.

In Jesus,
the religious power brokers were threatened
so they had to get rid of him.

Because in their book ... which certainly wasn't the Bible,
custom was more important than compassion,
tradition was more important than truth,
self-interest was more important than salvation.

It's not always easy to distinguish what we want, from what God
requires, especially if what God requires is costly.

JESUS DIED THROUGH *PHYSICAL CONSTRAINTS* reads the
first sign post.
Powerful people didn't like him.

*   *   *

Of course other people have died in similar style, Adolph Hitler
and Martin Luther King being two. But these deaths—of a ruthless dictator and a black prophet—have not had anything like the
same effect on the world as Jesus' death.

So why did Jesus die?

The second sign post has to read *FOR ME*

A hundred hymns and choruses spring to mind with phrases like,
'He died for my sake',
'In my place condemned he stood',
'His blood was shed for me',
'He took my place on Calvary's hill.'

How do we understand that Jesus died for me ... for us?
Let me follow his example and tell a story, a parable:

There was a weightwatcher's club in a certain city which you could only join if you were over twenty stone.

When it was established, the thirty or so participants agreed on some basic rules: they were going to be abjectly honest; they were going to admit the food they ate which they should have avoided; and they were each going to try to get to their target weight (the average weight for someone their age and size) within six months. For every excess pound, offenders would pay a penalty of one pound.

They started with great enthusiasm,
but as the weeks went on, will-power began to wane.

In the early days they would talk to each other seriously about their night excursions into the fridge in the kitchen or the box of Maltesers on the shelf at the foot of the bed, and savour the disapproval of each other's criticism.

But as the weeks went on,
they still admitted what they got up to,
but took it more casually, and sometimes even joked, about their misdemeanours.

The day of reckoning came
when, after six months, they all stood on the scales and discovered
how near or how far away they were from the ideal.

And when all the excess pounds of weight were added up, it was
discovered that among them they would have to pay a combined
penalty of around £2800.

They stood around, wondering who would be the first to write a
cheque for his or her proportion of the penalty. Nobody was keen
to take the lead. Then into the room came a man they all knew,
but who no one ever expected to see in their midst. He was the
thinnest man in the neighbourhood. He knew them all and one
by one he said their names:

'Alex, Jennifer, Marjory, Annette, Giles',

and then, with sad eyes … 'Have you no idea what you are doing
to yourselves?'

And then he, a poor man, took out his wallet and emptied his life
savings, £3000, into the kitty and went out.

Some people laughed at him.
Some people called him a fool.
And some people gave up over-eating for the rest of their lives.

* * *

It is not over-eating which is our dilemma,
it is the ability to sin.

The saintliest and the sourest of us knows that the good we mean to do, we don't do, and the evil we should avoid is what we turn our hand to. And the New Testament, keen that we should not have to select or narrow our understanding of sin by confining it to sexual behaviour rather than financial racketeering, is careful to list gluttony, avarice and malicious gossip alongside fornication.

The saintliest and the sourest of us know the reality of sin.

And sometimes when we are alone,
or as we lie in bed, or sit in a train,
we review our lives.
And if we think long enough
   on the harm we have done to ourselves,
   the ill with which we have affected others,
   and at times of our total disregard for the God who
    made us and calls us his own,
we wonder how this could ever be paid for …
      made up for …
      dealt with …
this sin … to which we are bound.

So Jesus came into the world,
the thin man,
the man who has no sin.

And seeing the collective guilt in which we all have a share
and our pathetic impotence to deal with the wrong we have done,
he says, 'Do you not see what you are doing to yourselves?'
and then he pays the penalty.

Jesus is not crucified by the sins of the world,

immediately evident in the lives of those
who sent him to Calvary,
as a helpless victim.

Jesus is crucified by his own consent.
He could have avoided the cross.
But he let himself be nailed to it.

For only thus could he show that God loves us so much …
that this is how far he'll go.

And also by allowing sin for the moment to get its way, can Jesus
in his resurrection prove that there is something mightier than
the power of sin.

That is the love of God which is meant for you
and you
and you.

Why did Jesus die?

The second signpost says
'FOR ME'
so that no longer do I need to be tied to sin.
I can be tied to the stronger chords of the
love of God.

*   *   *

There's a third signpost I want to point to, and it concerns the
text with which I began:

*Unless a grain of seed shall fall into the ground and die
it remains but a single grain.
But if it dies, it produces many grains.*

Why did Jesus die?

TO SET AN EXAMPLE.

For us who shiver when we see a hearse, death is a very final thing.
But not for Jesus.
He identified in nature, in a handful of seeds,
                              in one seed … a law of life.

It is only by dying that new life can come.

If a flower blossoms eternally, there is no growth. The flower has
to wither; the seed pod fall open, the seed become embedded in the
ground, so that next year there is not one flower, but ten in the
same place.
It was no use, Jesus just blooming all the time;
            no use, Jesus just making speeches about God's power;
            no use, Jesus just claiming that death was not the end.
People might admire his oratory, but he wouldn't take away their
fear, their shivers as the hearse went by.

Only by dying, and being raised to new life
and personally convincing his friends that death was not the end,
could he make his claims credible.

And you and I … sisters and brothers in Jesus,
you and I are invited by him to experience and demonstrate that
death is not the end, not by allowing ourselves to be nailed to a

cross as he was, but by allowing to die that which has to go in order that God can do something new.

When I was Youth Advisor in the Glasgow Presbytery, the importance of letting the grain of wheat fall to the ground and die became very clear on the first visit I ever made outside the office. I had a phone call from someone who asked if I would come to their church on Sunday night to see what could be done to revive their youth fellowship. I got off the bus and walked along to the church hall.

I groped my way along an unlit entrance till I found a back door. After hammering for five minutes, someone appeared.

I said who I was and was told people were expecting me.

I was taken upstairs to meet the 'Youth Fellowship'.
It consisted of four 23 year olds and one 30 year old, sitting in a row of hard wooden chairs, watching a kettle trying to boil on a gas ring and wondering why they had such small numbers.

I said, 'My dears, this is neither youth, nor is it fellowship
And I doubt very much if anything will ever happen for young people in this place, until you let this organisation die and allow God to do a new thing.'

If we believe in the resurrection …
    we have to allow some things to die.

God doesn't deal with corpses,
                with moribund institutions and lifeless people
                who linger or malinger, trying to avoid the end.

God deals with bodies which die and are raised to new life.

And it is perhaps only if in our personal lives,
> in relationships that are lifeless,
> in habits that are stale,
> in aspects of church life that are antiquated;
it is only if we allow such things to die, and discover that God
will give us new life, that when ultimately our own death approaches,
we will know, with Jesus, that it is not the end of the road,
> but the door to a new beginning.

5

Wrestle and Fight and Pray

Readings: Genesis 32:22-31; Matthew 10:34-42

Graham Hick and Graham Gooch,
Gabriela Sabatini and Steffi Graf,
Boris Becker and Michael Stich ... are *not* members of this con-
gregation.
But they are names which this congregation might know because
TV and radio tell them so.

This is the time of year when I turn on Radio Three to listen to
Tchaikovsky and hear thud ... thud ... thud; and while I'm wondering in which symphony the percussion is used so strangely,
an announcer tells me it's the West Indies at Trent Bridge.

Last week, in a flight of fancy,
I was wondering—in this sporting season—
to which sport Christianity might be most favourably compared.

Is it like cricket
which, from the outside looks absurdly dull,
but which the enthusiasts are keen to assure us is really exciting?

Or is it like tennis,
fairly predictable,
but with the word 'love' used in public from time to time?

Is it like golf,
something essentially easy—putting a ball into a hole—
until you see the size of the hole, the size of the ball
and how far away they are from each other?

Is it a team game, like rugby,
which needs people who are light on their feet up front
and people who are very solid to prop up the rear?

Or is it like snooker,
something which only a few folk can play very well,
but which has a vast army of armchair critics?

And then …
then I remember God's favourite sport
      which isn't any of the above,
      which doesn't require any special equipment like tennis,
      which doesn't involve mainly one part of the body
         like football,
      which doesn't have to be played at a special venue
         like ice hockey.

It's a sport which links such unlikely names as
                    Giant Haystacks
                    Mick McManus
                    and Paul of Tarsus … WRESTLING.

Now why it can be called God's favourite sport, I'll indicate below, but at this point I want to consider wrestling as the sport most analogous to Christianity—because as distinct from what others might say or we might think, to be a Christian is to be involved in struggling.

Language about fighting and struggling is present all through the Bible, though in more recent years and no doubt due to the change in public perception about the arms race, we don't use these words so often, and we don't sing hymns about soldiers and fighting as much as we did twenty years ago.

But still,
>   still at the heart of our faith
>   is the express intention of God that our religion should not be
>>   an opiate,
>>   a drug,
>>   an escape,

but an encounter in which we wrestle and fight and pray.

And to be specific
I want to look at three areas,
>>   arenas,
>>   rings, if you must,

in which we are enjoined to wrestle.

*   *   *

1. *WRESTLING WITH OURSELVES*

Implanted in each of us is a debating chamber without chairs where some of the fiercest arguments we experience take place and we witness them on our own.

And we call that debating chamber our conscience
>   the cause of sleepless nights, sometimes,
>   the cause of swithering over decisions, sometimes,
>   the mechanism which, without words,
>>   questions our actions,

        our desires,
        our inclinations …
in such a way as we end up wrestling internally.

But our consciences only work if they are informed.

Let me give you an example.
It has always amazed me that some people can sit down to a meal, pick at one or two vegetables, take a mouthful of meat and then set their knife and fork aside.

I, on the other hand, feel compelled to finish everything in front of me.
My conscience won't let me leave a dirty or a half-full plate.

Now why is this?

It's because when I was a wee boy,
I grew up in a family where money was scarce,
        where my mother was a good cook
        and where my father consistently reminded
me of the millions of starving children in the world.

Admittedly I sometimes prayed to God that my father would send my plate of tripe to the starving millions instead of compelling me to swallow it!

My upbringing has informed my conscience and allows for the healthy internal wrestling in later life.

Undoubtedly one of the reasons why we read the Bible and preach from it, one of the reasons why we learn about the teaching of

Jesus Christ, is not so that we can have a set of rules to live by, but so that our consciences can be informed by what is right.

And a magnificent thing about the Bible and about the teaching of Jesus, is that it informs our conscience

about duty to God	... yes
about prayer	... yes
about personal morality	... yes

but also about what our money is for,
who our compassion is for,
how rulers should govern,
and the intrinsic value of the created world.

Yet is it not the case, that most of us would wrestle with our consciences much more over skipping our bus fares (a sin not mentioned in the Scriptures) than in over-using detergent or petrol to the detriment of earth—the kind of abuse which is proscribed throughout the Bible?

We need to keep our consciences informed of all the purposes of God in order that we might wrestle with them.

*   *   *

2. *WRESTLING WITH COSMIC POWERS*

This is the second arena, the second ring in which we are expected to wrestle, and St Paul is the referee who summons us to combat.

In the sixth chapter of Ephesians, he says:
We are wrestling not against human foes,
but against cosmic powers,
against the authorities and potentates of this dark age,

49

> *against the superhuman forces of evil in the heavenly realm.*

Now the language may seem a bit obscure to us who do not live in a world surrounded by gods and idols in the way the people of Ephesus were. But while we might no longer believe that there are malignant powers in the skies desiring to create havoc on earth, I don't think we could deny that there is evidence around us of the forces of darkness.

I find St Paul's distinction very interesting.

He says, 'We are wrestling *not* against human foes
       but against cosmic powers.'

And I believe that this is of profound relevance to us who live in a world where the wrestling is too often against the human foes, and not enough against cosmic powers.

It struck me recently, as I was looking at newspapers, that our news has more and more to do with personalities, with people, and less and less, compared to the past, with issues. It is perhaps because we can relate more easily to a person ... we can say 'I like her' or 'I hate her' more easily than we can deal with complex issues.

Bertold Brecht, at the end of his play *The Resistible Rise of Alberto Ui*, illustrates our danger. The play is a parody of the rise and fall of Hitler. It ends with his assassination. Then, just as the audience feels relief, a poem appears projected on to a screen above the stage, a poem which ends with the words:

'the bitch which bore him
is still in heat'.

Hitler may be dead, the human foe dealt with, but Fascism, the cosmic power, still has to be wrestled with.

When, as last week, I meet someone who is caught up in the vicious spiral of heroin addiction, I may feel that the answer is to get them off the drug. I may even feel that I should inform on the pusher and have him or her imprisoned.

But if I am on the Lord's side, then following St Paul's injunction, my struggle has to go further. It has to do with the cosmic power of evil; it has to deal with the iniquity in high places. It has to address the fact that whenever in Western society people are put out of work, a propensity for alcoholism or drug addiction quickly follows. And that is a structural evil.

It has also to deal with the global trafficking in drugs, with cartels and triads which the international forces of justice have yet to quash.

It has to do with the iniquitous fact that peasants in Colombia and Peru harvest these drug crops with the permission of their government, because national debt is so extortionate that this is the only way that a poor person can make a living.

My fight is not just with the junkie, not just with the pusher,
        it is with the forces of evil.

If we are on the Lord's side,
        and we see pictures of famine and poverty eating away

at children in Ethiopia or the Sudan,
our response is not just to deal with the immediate
hunger by donating to Christian Aid.

Our struggle is to ask … why are the poor, poor?
How long can we pay farmers in Europe to keep fields
bare and import more food than we grow,
if our lands could be put to a better use—
to feed the hungry?

This is the uncomfortable wrestling we are summoned to, if we are
on the Lord's side.

*　　*　　*

3. *WRESTLING WITH GOD*
But there is a third arena, a third ring in which we are enjoined to
wrestle, a third kind of bout. Wrestling with the one for whom
wrestling is his favourite sport—God himself.

The story of Jacob which we read fascinates me the more I look
at it.

It opens with the information that Jacob had two wives.
(Depending of our experience of marriage, you might want to
 say 'Lucky Man!' or 'Poor Soul!')

It ends with an injunction to butchers not to sell certain meat
surrounding the sciatic nerve.

But the centre of the story is about a man, who, when alone, is
made to wrestle by a total stranger.

And the initiative is the stranger's not Jacob's.

This is not Job wrestling with his doubts
This is not Jeremiah wrestling with his anger
This is not Jesus wrestling in Gethsemane with his vocation.

This is God.
This is God who is the wrestler.
This is God who decides to intervene and upset.

It is not what we pray for!
(Whoever in their devotions asks God to upset them?)

It is not what we expect of God!
(We call Christ the Prince of Peace,
 not the Welter Weight Champion of the world.)

Yet God sometimes irrespective of our wishes chooses to engage
us in a struggle which we would rather avoid. Perhaps … perhaps in order that we might know him better.

The people whom I have come to love most dearly
are not necessarily the people who agree with me
or say yes to me every time.
Such people have only shown me what in them is like me.

The people I have come to love most dearly,
are those with whom I have argued, and disagreed,
who have said the things I did not want to hear
yet said them in love.
And through the dispute,
        through the struggling

I have learned more about them and have revealed more of my-self to them.

So God, in order that we may know him better,
has always the option to upset us,
to come not just as our friend
> but also as our antagonist
> and, as with Jacob, to bless us and make us vulnerable.

Some time ago, many of us were privileged to hear the group Mus-ica Para Todos from Argentina sing in a church in Glasgow ... no, not just sing ... *celebrate,* and move us so much that a rare thing happened—we unemotional Scots gave them a standing ovation.

During their stay in Scotland, I had a number of conversations with some of the group and was particularly impressed by one of them called Julio Lopez.

He had been brought up in a Pentecostal background, was con-verted at an early age and was an evangelical Christian all through the years of military dictatorship.

After Galtieri and his colleagues fell from power, Argentina began to take stock of what had happened. And one thing which had happened was that 30,000 men had disappeared. It was the regime's policy to lock up in secret concentration camps anyone suspected of disagreeing with government policy.

So, after Galtieri fell, the new government set up a commission to try to establish what had happened to these 30,000 disappeared men. The members of the commission were to take evidence from women who had lost their husbands, or whose sons had been removed in dawn raids. They had to listen to the testimony of men who had been in concentration camps and who had escaped. They had to listen to the guilt-ridden stories of soldiers who had brutalised their fellow countrymen.

And, in the middle of this, members of the commission had to try to find out names of who disappeared when,
>who was imprisoned with whom,
>who could be identified by a mark, an affectation, a speech defect.

Several members of the commission gave up because the agony of interviewing relatives of the disappeared was too much for them.

In an attempt to get other members, Julio Lopez was approached.
>'Oh no,' he said,
>'That has nothing to do with me.
>I am a Christian … I have other things to attend to.'

But in time Julio altered his opinion. He recounted, 'I was driving back from the meeting where I had been asked to become a member of the commission … and suddenly I heard God saying to me:
>'Julio …
>have the 30,000 disappeared nothing to do with me?
>Am I not a God who loves justice and hates oppression?
>Is the work of this commission not my work?'

So Julio changed his mind

But not just his mind …
>he had to change his theology;

     he had to understand that God was bigger than he imagined;
     he had to change his prayer life;
     he had to open his house.

Like Jacob he was blessed   … by a fuller knowledge of God
Like Jacob he was wounded … because he began to feel and
                           share the hurt of his people
                           which hitherto he had avoided.

Oh yes, our God loves to wrestle,
though our God is a God of Peace.
And those who experience his peace are those who
for him
and with him,
wrestle and fight and pray.

6

You are my Witnesses

Readings: Isaiah 44:1-8; 2 Timothy 1:8-14

Text:

> *You are my witnesses* (Isaiah 44:8).
> *Never be ashamed of witnessing for our Lord* (2 Timothy 1:8).

Like the Carruber's Close Mission in Edinburgh's Royal Mile, the Tent Hall in Glasgow was a great place for evangelical rallies.

It was run by pious Glaswegians who loved the Lord, and it catered for all types, especially for those society conveniently forgets.

It happened that one night in the 1940s, the Tent Hall was filled for a testimony meeting. Some had come to listen, some to enjoy the tea and iced buns which would be offered mid-evening.

Up to the lectern came a middle-aged woman whose face told stories of
where she had been,
what she had drunk,
and how she had been treated.

'Listen yous … ,' she began
'I'm no very good at public speaking.
I've never done it before.
But I've goat waan thing I want to tell yous.

'Last night I was in the arms of the devil
and tonight, I'm in the arms of the Lord.'

… at which point a drunk leaned over the balcony and shouted:

'And how are you fixed for tomorrow night, sister?'

That's the kind of story I enjoy, partly because I have never been a great enthusiast for public testimonies.

Most of them followed a pattern which is as tightly structured as a Latin Mass.

They tend to begin with a phrase such as:
'I wasn't brought up in a Christian home.'
or
'I used to go to Sunday School when I was a child
but then … '

The next movement is usually a description of the kinds of
debauchery,
excesses,
infidelities
and criminal acts in which the convert once took part, sometimes told in such compelling detail that the listener feels a bit like a voyeur.

Next is the section dealing with the time date and place of con-version, normally including a phrase such as

'I saw the light' or
'I met the Lord'

… though if you ask the convert, he or she will normally admit that this is the language of metaphor.

And finally there is the testimony to the changed life and to the good things that are now happening … 'I don't drink',

'I don't smoke',
'I don't gamble'.

Apart from the predictability of such testimonies, I find two things annoying.

The first is the smugness and sometimes spiritual arrogance of the outcome:

'I don't smoke',
'I don't drink',
'I don't gamble'.

Never mind the fact that the testifier regularly guzzles up gallons of fizzy lemonade which adds hyperactivity to arrogance … *I don't drink.*

Never mind that he or she might unnecessarily burn leaded petrol so both polluting the atmosphere and diminishing finite resources … *I don't smoke.*

Never mind that he or she (as was the case of a man I met quite recently) might play the stock market or the futures market … *I don't gamble.*

Second, I find such testimonies, despite their sincerity, somewhat deficient in comparison with biblical examples.

I have heard plenty of people testifying to the power of God which has assured them of a good measure of financial or material benefit; but very few who, like Matthew and Zacchaeus would have to say that their conversion led them to losing money rather than making it.

I've heard plenty avow how the Holy Spirit has given them the gift of tongues; but the same testifiers seem to lack the gifts of patience and gentleness which are also born of the Holy Spirit.

I've not really much time for testifiers.
Maybe like me you feel that they're better left out of parish churches
              better left to the Carrubers Close
              or the Tent Hall.

How smug,
how spiritually superior
how arrogant … *we are!*

*   *   *

Let me testify. I've been jolted out of that position of late, because of two things: the first was being confronted with the second letter of Timothy. In it Paul clearly says:

'Never be ashamed of witnessing for our Lord.'

And much as I like to think otherwise, I know that this is not an isolated verse. I know that elsewhere in 2 Corinthians, Paul encourages us to be 'Ambassadors for Christ.'

I know that the letter of Peter encourages us
                    'to be ready to give account for the hope
                    that is in us.'

I discover that in the Old Testament, prophets like Isaiah say that
                    God calls us to be witnesses.

And I remember that Jesus says that if we are ashamed
                    to witness for him on earth, he will refrain
                    from mentioning our name in heaven.

To be a witness ... to testify ... is a *scriptural injunction*. God
expects it of us.

But the other thing that jolted me from my recent arrogance was
meeting a man called Eddie McCreadie. I didn't know him, but he
knew me. He was dressed in denim shorts and training shoes, and
called to me across Great Western Road in Glasgow,

    'Haw big man!'

(... that's a term of endearment which Glaswegians use for any
male over 5 feet 6 inches.)

Then he crossed over the road and for twenty minutes he witnessed to me.
He told me how he hadn't been brought up in a Christian home;
                    how two of his brothers had died through misuse of
                    drink and drugs;
                    how he had been going the same way and was caught

up in organised crime;
how he had seen the light at an evangelical rally;
how he no longer drank,
but lived with and loved his wife and child.

And he was funny ... because he told of how,
when he spoke in tongues,
      people thought he was a headbanger;
      and he told of how he's been asked to leave churches
      because folk can't cope with his zeal for the Lord.

And I was moved.
I was very moved by this gallus Glaswegian with his impeccably
bad grammar.

He had been transformed ... and he knew by whom ... and there
was no denying it.

And I began to wonder ...
      is this word of Paul about witnessing for our Lord
      only to be taken up by those who have been rescued
      from skid row?

      Is testifying only for the ex con,
          the reformed gambler,
          the converted alcoholic?

      Is witnessing only for the gentiles ...
          and not for the genteel?
          only for the born-agains,
          and not for the comfortably liberal?

Ah … but some might argue:
we don't have to stand at a lectern, or speak in the street.
      Some of us witness by what we do.
      It's not what you say, it's how you live.
Undoubtedly true, but let's not wriggle.

We know what Paul means
       and Peter means
       and Isaiah means
       and Jesus means
when they call us to be witnesses,
       to testify;

they want a word said *for the Lord.*

And here we might recoil.

Can't we just have a conversations about our traditions,
       talk about Calvinism and Catholicism,
       have a discussion about the new ecumenical era?

Couldn't we have an argument about what the Bible says about
       divorce or euthanasia or the ordination of women?

We might even stretch as far as debating the niceties of the
assumption of the Blessed Virgin Mary or the doctrine of tran-
substantiation.

But all that,
       all that, important as it may be, is to get away from the
       '*res ipsa*' … the thing itself.

We are not asked to give an account of *what we know*
but of *whom we know*
and the one is not synonymous with the other.

*   *   *

When I was a student sharing a flat with another three people, we decided one Friday night to hold the kind of party students are presumed to have every weekend.

By ten o'clock, out of an invited guest list of fifty, all had appeared, plus twenty more. By midnight 140 had crammed into the third storey tenement flat.

At half past twelve there was a knock at the door and I answered it determined that no more should enter. I asked the boy standing in front of me who had invited him.

'John Bell,' he replied.

Not to miss an opportunity, I asked if he knew John Bell.
'Oh yes,' came the reply—and then the boy began to list a range of virtues and vices, some of which I could never aspire to and others I could never repeat.

'You know about him,' I said … 'but do you *know* him?'

'Why?' asked the boy, 'what difference does it make to you?'

'I am he,' I replied, much to his embarrassment.

We are expected not just to *know about* what we believe,

but to *know whom* we believe and to witness for him.

So how do we, who are not Tent Hall testifiers, begin to speak of *whom* rather than *what*?

It all hinges on us understanding that faith is to do with a relationship above all else. A person to person relationship, the person who God is to the person whom I am.

If you stand in a personal relationship to someone, you can say a word for them. If you only know about them from repute, you cannot testify.

And in development of this personal relationship on which all hinges, I want to mention two things which for *me* have become important. And I say for *me,* because it would be folly to preach on witnessing in the abstract.

*   *   *

The first is a commitment to prayer as a means of conversation, rather than a sequence of requests.

If you go to the doctor with a pain or a problem which has been bothering you for a while, you sometimes approach the surgery both with a prepared speech and with a clear request.

'It's my back, doctor.
I think I need some of these pills you gave Mrs McEwan.'

If your doctor is a wise doctor, he or she will not respond to your request, but will begin to talk about a range of things other than what you have said. And through the conversation you will be enabled to see that what is best for your condition might be very different from Mrs McEwan's pills.

And you will come away from that consultation speaking well of your doctor, not because she gave you what you wanted, but because she helped you realise what you needed, and also gave you an insight into how her own mind works.

Earlier this week, when I was coming down from Inverness, my mind went back to the last time I had been up North. I had been to Caithness and met a young elder whose minister had told me that he had been having a particularly hard time lately. His worries were compounded by discovering that his three year old child, Martin, had a cancerous growth in one ear and the prognosis was not good.

I had never met the child, but I felt for the plight of that family and I prayed for Martin for the next three months. When I got off the Inverness train and arrived home, I discovered among my mail a letter from the minister in Caithness from whom I hadn't heard since I met Martin's father in his company.

In his letter, almost as an afterthought, he mentioned that the cancerous growth in the wee boy had cleared up.

Now was that the power of prayer or the practice of medicine?

The cynic will debate that for hours!
Well, *let* the cynic debate it for hours.

But meanwhile, let some folk practise medicine and others

practise prayer in the knowledge that if the medicine fails, prayer succeeds ... not in producing longed-for miracles, but in enabling us to discern the will of God and relate to him.

I stress the primary objective of prayer is not a miracle.

I was very impressed last week when I met a woman who had lost her second husband through a heart attack, which is what her first husband died of eight years previously.

I had expected she might be angry,
                  might be annoyed that her prayers for her
                       husband's recovery
                  had evidently gone unheeded by heaven.

But no ... because her prayer was not of the direct request variety, but was like the patient conversing with the doctor: she was able to see into the will of God and say, with assurance, that for her husband, his death was his healing.

The prayer in which we converse with God about what we want and argue or discuss with him what he wants, is the activity which enables us to know whom we have believed, and to be as unembarrassed about saying a word for him as we would if we were speaking about a friend.

*   *   *

The second activity which I believe allows us to witness, is to live out God's word.

The garrulous witness from Maryhill was able to indicate what changes had happened in his life because he had taken the promise of Jesus Christ seriously that his sins could be forgiven, would be forgiven, that all things could be, and would be, made new.

And he could measure the difference,
> measure the growth,
> note the changes,
> and proudly confess the one who had made these changes possible.

Now ... if I were to leave this pulpit, and in the style of a chat-show host come into the congregation with a microphone and ask what difference Jesus Christ had made in your life in the past year ... would you have an answer?

If our relationship with God is dynamic, then things will have happened because we took this word or that word seriously. If our relationship is static then we will feel today and act today much the same as we did last year at this time.

The scriptures of the Old and New Testament were not written so that they might one day be read in public in churches and expounded by a succession of preachers, but so that through them we *all* might take seriously who God is,
> what God requires of us,
> and so that we might act on our knowledge
> and be able to measure the difference.

I'm not suggesting for a moment that we should swallow Genesis to Revelation, hook, line and sinker.

I am suggesting that we take one, just one word from the Lord

and become so familiar with it … now … yes, why not right now?
… until we are able to measure the difference.

And for some that might be Psalm 23:
>'The Lord is my Shepherd
>I shall not want
>I shall *NOT* want.'

And for some that might be Psalm 13:
>'How long O Lord will you forget me
>How long?
>How *LONG*?'

For some it might be Jesus' word to his disciples:
>'Don't let your heart be weary
>*DON'T* let your heart be weary.'

And for some it might be another word:
>'I came to bring a sword
>*I* came to bring a sword.'

It is by living out such words,
>by interacting with them,
>by being moved by them, that we will be able to measure
the difference, just as it is by persevering in prayer, we will be able
to converse with our Maker.

And then, maybe not in the Tent Hall
>but in a higher or humbler place
>we will be able to say with the saints
>and with Eddie McCreadie,
>>'I know *WHOM* I have believed.'

69

7

On Death and Dying

Readings: 1 Corinthians 15:12-22; John 12:20-28

At the turn of the century in the village of Crookedholm, near Kilmarnock, a commercial traveller was watching a group of children playing at funerals.

At the front of a solemn procession came a wee boy walking slowly with something like a hat stuck on his head. He was the undertaker.

Behind him came two boys, their hands tucked under their chins, their backs arched as if straining … these were the horses. Then came four boys delicately carrying a wee girl who had agreed to be the corpse and they the cortege.

And behind them was a sorry procession of children snivelling into their handkerchiefs or wiping their faces with their shirt sleeves. These were the mourners.

Thinking that he would play along with the children, the traveller approached one of the first children to pass him and said quietly,

'Wha's deid?'

... to which came the solemn reply,

'How should I ken? ... I'm jist a horse!'

Sometimes I can hear or tell that kind of story and sympathise with the child who didn't know who the procession was for, because sometimes I seldom see a hearse or attend a funeral.

And then, at other times, I feel that I associate with John Donne's line.

'*Ask not for whom the bell tolls ....*'

not because it necessarily tolls for me,
but it might be tolling for someone known to me.

This is the situation in which some of us find ourselves from time to time—aware of the randomness of mortality, aware of an end to breathing.

Not long ago some of us found ourselves between two memorial services: the one, a Saturday afternoon in Govan Old
celebrating the long life of George MacLeod,
justifiably filled with love, laughter, sentiment
and irreverence, as he was;
and perhaps a distant reflection of the colourfulness
of his reception into heaven:

the other, a week later,
not for an old man in his nineties,
but for a young man in his thirties,
Graham Aitken, Glasgow Presbytery's Youth Adviser,

a lovely, vital, attractive, dynamic young Christian, husband, father, mown down by a car while cycling to his work.

Later the following week, came the news of the death of two very rare people, Mark and Lottie Cheverton, in their thirties. They set up an independent art school in Edinburgh to motivate a wide range of people who thought they couldn't draw. They had magnificent successes. They were devoted Christians. And they were involved in a crash in which they both died.

And you wonder … you wonder … what kind of world is it … and what kind of God is it who allows one veteran prophet and pacifist to last almost a century, and three young people in their prime, with their devoted lives just beginning to bear fruit, to be cut down.

Phrases like 'only the good die young' are no comfort.

There's an injustice in it all, maybe a double injustice.

Why does God let one person outlive his usefulness, a man who had completed his life's work—and why cut others off in their prime?

But more, why should those who never give a tinker's curse for the Lord Jesus Christ and the establishment of the Kingdom of God be spared, and those who are devoted servants be separated in death from all that they could have done and all they were doing for this same kingdom?

One of the very discomforting things that we have to cope with is that whatever else it is, the Christian faith is not an inoculation against road accidents, cancers, persecution and death.

Much though we might like it to be so, much as we hope fervently it might be, when we say our prayers for our safety and the safety of our families, God seems to give us even treatment with the most hideous of heathens when it comes to accident and illness.

Though truth to tell, if we read our Bibles, that is not a new insight.

The Bible has scarcely begun when Cain kills Abel … a man in whom God was well pleased; Samson, for no evil in him, gets his eyes gouged out and dies in his prime; David loses an infant child and then his son Absalom; Stephen, hardly a year into his discipleship, gets stoned to death.

It would seem that Christians are treated no different by God from other folk when it comes to death and danger. There is no insurance policy, no ethereal safety-net preventing us from falling off a cliff or falling under the wheels of a car.

So how are we to respond? … when disaster strikes.
Have we just to grin and bear it, say it's a hard life?

I want to suggest *not* the answer, or even a clue to the answer, of the mystery of hideous suffering or untimely death. But I do believe that there are distinctive ways in which Christian people should respond.

The first is with *anger*.

*　　*　　*

If someone we love dies suddenly,
                is killed,
                is diagnosed as having a fatal illness,
and we feel aggrieved at this, angry about it,
then the last thing we should do is put on a mask of false piety.

We should be angry!
We should complain to God!
We should ask why?
And we should not be afraid to do that.

For God is not some fragile doll who will fall off his perch if our voice or our temper rises.

And no one,
      no one in the Bible was ever given a row by God for being justifiably angry.

If that were the case, Jeremiah would have been struck down a hundred times for arguing with the Almighty.

If it were the case that God didn't like complaints, a third of the Psalms would never have been written.

If Jesus had no time for people complaining, then when Mary came to see him and said, 'Lord, if you had been there, my brother would not have died!', Jesus would have told her to shut up and get on with her life.

But no, what does he do? ... He listens to Mary's anguish, anger,
                sorrow,
                he sees her tears

and then he cries himself.

God only enters into grief when we share that grief with him.

To refuse to grieve,
to suppress anger,
to avoid shouting at heaven the things we mumble on earth,
is to keep God out.

When bad things happen to good people,
when the innocent get mowed down like Graham Aitken,
we express our outrage … to let God in.

*   *   *

The second response I suggest that Christian people make to the mystery of undeserved suffering and death, is to put it in the context of other mysteries.

And it is the story of Job which most convinces me of this.

The story of Job is too long to abbreviate here, but it's worth a read. Job is a man who is successful, prosperous and devout. And in the course of a day, everything collapses around him—his family, his business, his home—all are destroyed and he is left desolate, engulfed by the mystery of undeserved suffering, unmerited disaster.

It's not until you get to the end of the book of Job that you begin to get a clue as to any hope of resolution.

At the end of the book, God speaks to Job directly.
And he doesn't say to him,

'Here's the answer to why you lost your family and business and fortune.'

Instead, God asks Job questions:

> Do you know the source from which light comes?
> Have you ever ordered the dawn to break?
> Do you know who laid the cornerstone of the world?
> Have you ever seen the storehouses of snow?

Question after question God piles on Job;
question after question … about the mysteries
>> of the world,
>> of the universe,
>> of the sun, moon and stars,
>> of wildlife.

And gradually Job becomes aware,
that the only way to deal with the mystery of suffering
is to see it in the context of the mystery of life.

We do not ask why the sun rises.
We only for a moment marvel at the birth of another unique human being.
We rarely stand back in amazement at the ingenuity of the human mind.
And so we lose our sense of mystery about all of human life, except death.

Death is no more mysterious than birth.
Suffering is no more mysterious than love.

That is what the cross is all about.

There we have Christ … strung up,
                        cut off in his prime,
                        persecuted when only thirty-three,
                        sentenced to a cruel death for doing good.

Oh, how utterly, utterly wrong … and why?

God doesn't supply the answers,
but in the midst of the mystery of Christ's suffering,
comes the mystery of God's love.

'Father forgive them' … and he means it.

It is not just tragedy that we don't deserve.
It is not sudden bereavement that we don't deserve.

We don't deserve the love of God!

But it's there, that unfathomable mystery to hold on to
        when we are grasped by other mysteries.

I suggest we complain … get angry
I suggest we put the mystery of death beside the mystery of birth,
the mystery of undeserved pain beside the mystery of unmerited
love.

But finally, if I might borrow some language from George MacLeod,
I believe it is distinctly Christian to live as those who have already
been measured for their shrouds, and who are not worried about
when the undertaker will come.

You and I, sisters and brothers,
when we belong to Jesus Christ,
belong to one who, though he was God's only Son, died.

And he died so that whoever believes in him should know that
they also will die.

And then he came out of the grave, dancing, so that all who believe
in him might know that when they draw their last breath they are
not going to remain still forever, but take part in the great process
we call resurrection.

The Gospel of our Lord does not say that we will *not* die.
It says we will die.
But God has taken care of that process.
It's in his hands,
and those who live in imitation of Jesus
                    will die as Jesus died
                    and will also rise to new life as he did.

So, for the Christian
there should be no need to fear death or dying.
Let us today be measured for our shrouds
and tomorrow book the funeral tea, even though it might not
happen for fifty years.

These things should hold no fear.
The worst thing is not to die.
The worst thing for a Christian is to disbelieve Jesus Christ,
                    who said, 'I am the resurrection and the life',
                    and who meant it.

8

Eyes fixed on Jesus

Readings: Hebrews 12:1-13; Matthew 14:22-23

Text: Hebrews 12:2

> *Let us keep our eyes fixed on Jesus, on whom faith depends*
> *from beginning to end.*

The German theologian, Dietrich Bonhoeffer, used to advise his
students that when they were going to preach from a difficult
text, they should let the congregation know.

That's the advice I take to heart in this address, because the passage on which I want to reflect may be considered by some to be
difficult;
>by others incredible;
>by others most extraordinary in the extreme.

It's the passage in Matthew's Gospel chapter 14 which describes
a curious incident which took place on the Sea of Galilee—in
which Jesus walks on water. Here is the latter portion of the story.
And before I continue, I'd like to read the passage again.

> *Then Peter spoke up. 'Lord, if it is really you, order me to*
> *come out on the water to you.' 'Come!' answered Jesus. So*

Peter got out of the boat and started walking on the water to Jesus. But when he noticed the strong wind, he was afraid and started to sink down in the water. 'Save me, Lord!' he cried. At once Jesus reached out and grabbed hold of him and said, 'How little faith you have! Why did you doubt?'

It has all the makings of a good thriller:
the incident happens at night … in the wee small hours;
> it happens at sea … with all the mystery of the deep at hand;
> it involves what seems like a supernatural appearance;
> there's screaming and shouting;
> there's a near death experience and a rescue;
> there's a happy ending with an edge on it.

In the hand of Alfred Hitchcock, it might make a film which would fill the cinemas, but preached in a sermon it runs the risk of emptying the churches.

We don't mind belief being suspended in the cinema while the camera plays tricks. We can perspire freely and then go home with a bag of chips, knowing it was just a film, nothing more.

But are we, in church, also expected to suspend our belief? Do we have to believe that this curious episode is credible?

*   *   *

Let me at the outset, tell you where I stand.

If you were to ask if I believe the facts of the story as recounted in Matthew's Gospel, I would reckon ninety per cent of me says yes … and 10 per cent doubts.

I'm not a credulous kind of person. I'm curious about what seems unbelievable. But what makes be believe the facts of this story is what happened to Grace Offalah.

Grace Offalah was the first black woman I ever had as a friend.

She came across to Scotland from Nigeria in the autumn of 1968 to start her training as a nurse. She lived in the next room to me in bedsitting accommodation in Great George Street.

In 1970 Grace told a story about how the first October she had been in Scotland, she was at a party in a friend's house. It was late at night and the doorbell rung. Because the friend was in the kitchen, Grace went to answer the door and when she did, she let out a yell and ran back into the living room screaming, 'It's a ghost! It's a ghost!'

Her friend went to the door and came back to reassure Grace that what she saw was not, in fact, a ghost. She then told her about what happened in Scotland at Hallowe'en.

Grace used to tell the story against and about herself, how she screamed with fright and was later reassured. And it follows much the same pattern and expresses much the same emotions as Matthew's story.

The Gospel narrative sounds like a story that people would tell against themselves. But it also has the hallmarks of authenticity regarding how Jesus and the disciples relate to each other.

He leaves them on their own at risk, while he goes alone to pray— that happens elsewhere.

They go out in a boat themselves—they do that elsewhere.
Peter is keen to do a wee bit of showing off—perfectly in character.
Jesus, in a moment, is able to give Peter both a hand and a telling
off—absolutely typical behaviour.

Add to that the fact that in this story of great poignancy St Matthew
criticises the disciples, while normally Matthew is keen to defend
them. At every turn, the credibility of the story grows and grows.

If you asked if I believe the facts of the story, ninety per cent of me
says it happened exactly as written.

But then I would want to say that, in a much deeper way, I *believe*
in this story one hundred per cent. Because this story was never
written to boggle the scientific, cynical minds of twentieth century
men and women. This story was written and recounted to nourish
the faith of men and women in every age.

And I believe that it is one of the truest stories in all of the Gospels
when it comes to offering insight into the human predicament.

The astounding thing about the story is not, NOT that Jesus walked
on water.
That is almost taken for granted in the narrative.
The most astounding thing about the story is that *Peter* walked on
water.

And how he walked on water is clearly stated … he looked at Jesus.
And how he began to sink is clearly stated too … he looked at the
waves.

That, in a cameo, represents the human predicament: that when we are confronted with the One for whom all things are possible, including walking on water, we turn our eyes away from him and become so terrorised and distracted by the things around us that we begin to sink.

*   *   *

Do you remember the days when you were first fascinated by Jesus Christ?
Do you remember the days when you took seriously what he said before what anybody else said and discovered that what he said had a truer and deeper ring to it?

Do you remember the days when—albeit for a short time—you believed that to come to worship in church was really to approach the gates of heaven: and that things could happen, things could change in the company of God's people; and they did?

Do you remember when you took seriously the command to love your neighbour and you actually tried it, and you stopped crossing the road to avoid the one you didn't want to meet, and in doing so you sensed that this really was the way to live?

Do you remember the days when you took to heart all the words in Scripture about God's burning passion for justice,
about Christ's clear desire that the hungry should be fed,
about the Holy Spirit's manifest ability to turn selfish affluent middle class pillars of the temple into generous socially aware Christians;
and so you got in on the act,
either collecting for Christian Aid,
or writing to your MP

or praying fervently
for an end to the war in Aden,
                            in Vietnam or whatever,
because God was a God of peace, and you sensed somehow that
this was more real,
more important than the thousand other things that demanded your
attention?

And being so fascinated by Jesus Christ,
      being so engrossed in his kingdom,
      being so convinced of his love,
you walked on water.

And then …
and then …
        you looked at the waves,
        you became aware of the worries,
        you thought the task was too big and you were too small,
        you heard the voices of those who said 'You don't believe
            that nonsense',
        you saw that the more you did the more there seemed to be
            yet to do,
        like Michel Quoist, the wider you opened the door, the more
            folk wanted to come into your life;

        and inside voices began to say
            'There isn't enough time!'
            'There isn't enough money!'
            'There isn't enough energy!'
            'There isn't enough love!'

and then … 'Help me, Jesus … I'm drowning!'

That's our predicament …
>WE KNOW WHO WE SHOULD LISTEN TO
>WE KNOW WHO WE SHOULD LOOK AT,
>BUT WE BECOME OBSESSED BY THE WAVES,
>AND WE SINK.

*   *   *

This story, the story of Peter walking on the water, makes quite clear two facts about our Christian existence:

The first is that *God lets folk sit in a boat on rough seas.*
The Gospel is not a safe harbour from the storm.
Jesus ended up getting crucified, not wrapped in cotton wool.

But the second fact of our Christian existence is that in the middle of whatever rough seas we are surrounded by, we have a clear choice. We have to decide who is going to fascinate and feed us—the waves, or the one who walks on them.

I want to apply this story to two aspects of the life you and I share.

The first is to do with the way we regard and talk about the Church, because in the present day there's enough bad news for us all to dine out on:

>there are plenty of forecasts of failure;
>there are plenty of horror stories;
>there is enough cynicism around to fill the columns of
>the newspapers from now till Doomsday.

And certainly, simply to be in the church and to look round and realise that only ten per cent of the seats are taken, is to encourage the question as to whether it's worth persevering.

But the Kingdom of God doesn't grow as we tell each other what seems to be wrong and spread the news in the world outside that we are sinking fast.

I was recently chairing a meeting of people who do a fair bit of complaining about the Church, and before we began the business, I asked them each to tell a story about something positive that had happened in their recent experience.

One by one they told their stories ... stories about things they had discovered, about changes in their church life which had worked, about people who had begun to think about the Christian faith for the first time, stories about being surprised by the goodness of God.

Then I asked, 'Why do you never share these things naturally? Why is it that we would much sooner complain, groan about the things that have gone wrong?'

Jesus Christ does not inhabit our pessimism.
Make no mistake.
Jesus Christ and his Spirit do not inhabit our pessimism and if negative carping and lamenting is all we share with the world outside, then we deserve to drown. Jesus Christ and his Spirit do not inhabit our pessimism, but are recognised in growth and change and in signs of goodness.

When we speak or think of the Church
        ... are we looking at the waves

or the one who is walking on them?

*   *   *

Second, I want to apply this story to our personal prayer life.

I read a magnificent book by Jock Dalrymple, who was a Catholic priest in Edinburgh. It's called *Simple Prayer* and I recommend it to anyone who is struggling with their devotional life.

In it the author puts his finger on how many of us, me included, normally approach prayer …
> as something which we have to do for God,
> as something which we have to get right,
> as a kind of memory test of all the people and troubles that need to be mentioned.

And so we besiege God's ears with our requests;
> we rehearse over and over again our failures;
> we become over conscious of what we're saying
> and how we're saying it
> and how long it's taking.

We concentrate on the waves and we are slowly sinking.

So obsessed are we with our voice and our condition that we are totally unaware that in prayer we can come into touch with another voice,
> deeper than our anxieties,
> deeper than our worries,
> deeper than our sense of inadequacy,
> deeper than our troubled conscience,

deeper than our stop-watch mind.

We are totally unaware that in the midst of our sea of uncertainty
there is one who is walking on the waves of our
troubled existence;
who wants us just to look at him
and see him reach out to us
and say to each of us as if we were the only one:

'I know you
I want you
I love you.'

Let us keep our eyes fixed on Jesus on whom faith depends from
the beginning to the end.

9

Unclean

Readings: Leviticus 13:1-8, 45-46; Mark 1:40-45

All through the centuries the Church has been guarded, guided and blessed by the Holy Trinity, Father, Son and Spirit. And through the same centuries the Church has been beleaguered, misguided and cursed by an unholy trinity of human devising—the ambiguous association of sin with disease and uncleanness.

This sorry inheritance which reappears in new guises in every age is the direct result of reading the Old Testament in isolation from the New.

It is an impression we might have received had we only concentrated our minds on the passage read earlier from Leviticus in which we find that anyone who has a diseased scab, or anyone from whom blood flows due to sickness, is not to be numbered among the ill, but to be called unclean. The next move from uncleanness to sinfulness is only a few steps away.

Lepers were to be avoided, and anything or anyone they touched was considered to be contaminated.

Women too, particularly during menstruation, were looked upon as being under the curse.

Behind this, though we don't always remember it, was the ancient belief that life resided in the blood. And therefore anyone who in any way was losing blood, whether by injury, haemorrhage or menstruation was considered to be engaged in a life-denying or sinful act.

This belief is not just an ancient one. It has its contemporary expression in, for example, the opposition to women being ordained.

I remember (and it's only fifteen years ago) being approached by a distressed divinity student in the Glasgow University who had just been hustled into a corner by three pious male counterparts. They said that God had told them to tell her not to pursue her vocation to the ministry.

> 'Why?' she asked them.
> 'Well … you've had children, haven't you?'
> 'Yes,' she answered.
> 'Therefore you are unclean.'

Old beliefs, old superstitions die hard, especially those which have been culled from a reading of the Old Testament apart from the New.

*   *   *

The Gospel story has hardly opened, indeed in Mark's Gospel, the first chapter has hardly ended, when Jesus is discovered to be in open conflict with conventional wisdom about the unholy alliance of sin, disease and uncleanness.

It is a leper who approaches him, a leper who should have stayed in his own colony, a leper who, according to biblical tradition, should have shouted UNCLEAN, UNCLEAN.

Instead he says, 'Sir, if you will … *you* can make me clean.'

And what does Jesus do?
> Keep back to avoid getting contaminated?
> Tell the leper that, as there were still visible signs
> of the disease on his body,
> he shouldn't come near a holy man?

> Tell Judas, who kept the common purse,
> to give the man a penny,
> or rather to put the coin on the ground
> and let the man pick it up?

When Jesus sees the man, he does three things:

First, he expresses anger. Why exactly, we don't know. But we may be sure it wasn't the anger of one who was annoyed at being interrupted by a leper. More likely he would be angry that such a vile disease should have so disfigured a child of God. Far rather he might have been angry because, in addition to the disfigurement, there was a forced isolation from the rest of society.

Second, Jesus to the alarm of his disciples, to the disgust of his critics, and to the delight of the lawyers who would both want to see him contaminated and be glad to charge him with breaking the law … Jesus reaches out and touches the man, with no thought for history or hygiene.

91

And third, with a word, he cures the man and sends him on his way.

Here, in this three-fold activity
of showing concern   (Anger),
of showing acceptance   (Touching),
of showing compassion   (Healing),
Jesus provided the model which he is to use elsewhere, whenever he is confronted with the unholy trinity of sin, uncleanness and disease.

Is this not what happens when he is approached by the woman who is haemorrhaging?

The disciples want her to be banished:
he wants her to be brought forward.

They want her reprimanded for touching him:
he wants her to be congratulated.

They consider her a hopeless case …
she has had all the medicine money can buy:
he cures her.

Is this not what happens when he is confronted with a man blind from birth?

His critics are convinced the man or his parents must have been sinners:
Jesus is annoyed with the way the man is disregarded.

They want him to remain blind:

Jesus wants him to see again.

They question Christ's credentials:
he gives him his sight.

Showing concern.
Showing acceptance.
Showing compassion …
> this is Christ's threefold response to the unholy trinity
> of sin, uncleanness and disease.

*   *   *

Churches in Glasgow, as churches all over the world, have been encouraged to mark World Aids Day … to mark it on the first Sunday in Advent when we remember a nation waiting for the fulfilment of God's promise to bring deliverance.

The subject is all but simple, and to take a facile stance on such a complex issue is not to act in the manner of Christ.

In Glasgow, people are dying of Aids.
If you don't know any, that doesn't mean the disease doesn't exist or affect you. I don't know anyone who has been murdered in the past year in the city, but I'm aware from the court reports that not every street is safe.

If this were Harare or Lusaka, we might be a bit more alarmed.

Two weeks ago, I was in the company of a couple whose daughter is working in a hospital in Zimbabwe. That morning she had phoned home and in the conversation had revealed how, in her hospital, a random blood test was made on twenty-five male patients. Twenty-one out of the twenty-five were discovered to be HIV positive.

And sad as that is for the men,
how much sadder for the women who in innocence might bear children, HIV positive from the womb.

And sad as that is for the women,
how much sadder for the children and adults who are haemo-philiacs and who become infected by bad blood.

Of course we can point the finger … though where the finger points keeps shifting.

> We can blame it on homosexuals who pursue what some would call an unnatural life style. But why should it affect male homosexuals and not female?

> We can blame it on the black men because so many of them in Africa are infected. But who is to say that black men introduced the disease to Africa? Viruses are colour blind.

> We can blame it on junkies, on people who share needles. But shall we also blame governments which allow unem-ployment to soar, knowing that historically wherever that happens, people turn to drink or drugs for release?

> And shall we blame it also on those who have so indebted Southern nations that sharing needles is the custom in Third World hospitals? There is just no money available for the kind of health care we enjoy.

We can blame it on the Blood Transfusion Service for not properly screening donations in the blood bank. But how were they to know about a disease which sometimes takes ten years to reveal itself?

But in any case,
let me ask you this.

From what you know of Jesus Christ,
from what you read in the Gospels,
from all you have ever learned of the Son of God,
do you think that the prime concern in Christ's heart is who is to blame?

What is the cross about,
if it is not the result of people looking at each other to find a scapegoat for their own inadequacy and wrongfulness?

Christ steps into the middle of our mess, into the middle of our seeking for a scapegoat and says,

'I'll take the blame …
because if I deal with the blame,
you might be able to discover the cure.'

Oh yes, let me not delude you,
sin and irresponsible, immoral behaviour
surround the disease we call AIDS …

just as sin and irresponsible, immoral behaviour
surround the diseases we call FAMINE, APARTHEID and POVERTY.

But two things have to be said:

First of all, with the issue of AIDS, we are dealing with diseased people and with a deadly virus.

And even if you want to consign to hell every homosexual, adulterer, and intravenous drug abuser, that doesn't deal with the virus. The virus is not under the microscope of morality or theology. The virus is under the microscope of medical research in the hope that it may be eradicated. And our prayers, as our money, should be with those who research in this important field.

And second ... if ... if we are Bible-believing Christians ... but only *if*, then we must see, as Karl Barth was keen to protest, that the first word of the Gospel is not about the supremacy of sin, but about the supremacy of the forgiveness of God.

Jesus was not primarily concerned to tell people that they were sinners. Folk knew that they had done wrong. He told them that God could forgive, restore, make new—and that is what converted them.

On this day when the world's attention is drawn to the AIDS issue, I wonder whether in your life and mine we might exhibit something of the character of Christ.

I wonder if we might, like him, show our concern, our anger, our outrage at a disease which disfigures children of God and at the circumstances which cause that disease to prosper.

I wonder, if we, like him, might either by our hands or by the hands of others, show acceptance ... and do that not just to people who are diseased, but to people who may become diseased if we want to perpetually quarantine those who reveal that their sexuality or their background or their race as not of a kind with which we feel comfortable.

I wonder if we, like Jesus, might be able by the skill of some, by the kindness of others, and by the prayers of all, to find a way of healing relationships,
> self-esteem
> and bodies.

And this is not something just for the young.

When I was in Belgium recently, I met a woman who went to a city centre Roman Catholic church, a church into which strangers often come. One of them, a man in his late twenties, visited and stayed, was warmly welcomed into the congregation and made the church his spiritual home.

Two years after he arrived, he revealed that he was HIV positive and soon after he developed AIDS. He was disowned by his parents, but not by his church. Every week, when he was in hospital, and until his death, the lady I met, whose name was Gabbie, visited him to hold his hand and to pray.

At the funeral, the man's mother appeared. Gabbie told her that he had died a peaceful death and that he had died a Christian.

And who had let him have a peaceful death, who had nourished his faith?

Gabbie de Wil is 79 … three times the age of the man who died.

Hers, as ours, was the ministry of concern and compassion and healing, which is primarily the ministry of Jesus Christ.

10

May they be the One

Readings: Ephesians 4:1-6; John 17:9-21

Text: John 17:21

May they be one, that the world might believe.

During the Week of Prayer for Christian Unity, I wanted to talk about prayer, an issue which I have not always felt comfortable with, perhaps because of the way in which I was introduced to it.

As a boy, my early devotions did not consist of saying the Rosary under a picture of the Sacred Heart. My childhood prayer consisted in repeating certain words under the watchful eye of my mother. I remember these words well:

> *This night as I lie down to sleep,*
> *I pray the Lord my soul to keep.*
> *If I should die before I wake,*
> *I pray the Lord my soul to take.*

I would want no one to be taught that prayer now as a child. I suppose I only learned it because there were no options. But it could have been very damaging because it depicts God as a kind of celestial snoop. Santa Claus comes down the chimney to give presents to little children while they are sleeping, But God ... God comes into the house in order to take away your soul before you wake!

The prayer might well have had its origins in the days when lots of children died in their early years and some comfort had to be offered to their brothers and sisters, but I don't know if it has any relevance today.

I never knew much about how Roman Catholics said their prayers until I went to university and at the age of eighteen discovered, in my first year, that to get an MA, I would have to take a class in that most unprotestant of subjects, Latin.

When it came to the first term examination, I was fascinated to find myself sitting diagonally across from a budding Jesuit, a product of good Catholic education who had, set out before him on the examination desk, a picture of the Virgin, a crucifix and a picture of another saint who, kicking with the right foot, I was unable to identify.

When the invigilator told us to proceed, while the rest of the class read the questions and avidly began translating into Latin a paragraph which looked like the Times editorial, my Roman friend to the right crossed himself, said a prayer, crossed himself again and proceeded in this way for a good six or seven minutes.

When the examination results were announced, I was astounded to discover that he had achieved seventy-six per cent and I had only managed twenty-three. For the next fortnight, I wondered whether I should become a Roman Catholic. There seemed to be educational benefits!

How Anglicans prayed, I never knew until fairly recently.

I was looking at material in an Anglican Bookshop when I came across a religious postcard. It depicted a very pious young female Anglican on her knees at the side of her bed. A bubble placed above her head indicated the substance of her prayer—

> Dear God,
> thank you very much for giving me a nice face,
> but is there something you could do about my fat bum?

It would, of course, be preposterous to claim that these three examples are representative of the kind of prayers which all, Protestants, Catholics and Anglicans, pray. I can hardly imagine the Pope asking God to get him through his Latin examination. And, having met the Archbishop of Canterbury, I know he's sufficiently slim not to have to ask God to do something about his fat bum.

But these three prayers, caricatures though they may be, illustrate what are often priorities when we address the Almighty. They have to do with …
> my soul,
> my success,
> my body.

And while this is true of most days when life is calm, it is doubly true of days when life is hard.

I don't imagine that there is anyone here who will have had the experience of being rushed to hospital in the middle of the night in a speeding ambulance, with blue lights flashing, siren blaring.

I had that experience once, and I hope I never have it again.

I can assure you that what prayers passed through my mind then
were not principally about Northern Ireland or Nicaragua,
            about the hungry in Ethiopia or the
            persecuted in South Africa,
            even about my family and my friends.

I was praying about me … about my life, which might not last
much longer … and I imagine that put in a similar situation, you
might do likewise.

… which makes Jesus' prayer very different and very peculiar.

I refer to the prayer which Jesus said not long before his arrest, the
prayer he said while his enemies were crossing their fingers and
Judas was contemplating what he might buy with thirty pieces
of silver; the prayer which Jesus uttered knowing that within
twenty-four hours he would be arrested, tried, found guilty,
sentenced and executed.

And in this extreme moment,
        in these dire straits,
what does he pray about … his soul?
                        his success?
                        his body?

No.

He prays for us.

He prays for his disciples, and, more than that,

> for all those who will put their trust in him
> because of what the disciples say.

He prays for those who will become Christians through the likes
of Peter and Paul,
> and thereafter through Ninian and Columba
>> through Theresa and Bernadette,
>> through Aloysius and John Ogilvy,
>> through John Knox and Mary Slessor,
>> and through all the humbler saints who
>> have influenced our lives for good and
>> for God.

On his road to death,
at the very moment when every mortal prays
for what is really important,
Jesus reveals what is really important to him—
that his disciples should express unity:

> 'Father, may they be one in us,
> as you are in me and I am in you,
> so that the world may believe it was you who sent me.'

Sadly, it seems to have taken us until the twentieth century to pay
more than lip service to this deep, deep desire of Jesus, to see
that heeding this prayer is not an option but an obligation.

When I was a teenager, loving Roman Catholics or expressing
unity with them was not important. That, in my upbringing, had
little or nothing to do with being a Christian.

It never dawned on me that I might learn something from the

Roman Catholic tradition. Indeed, it was frequently suggested to me that Roman Catholics were not Christians. They were to be spat on from the school bus, not embraced as equal in the eyes of God. It never dawned on me that when Jesus asked us to love one another, it meant loving 'them'.

Thank God things have changed and are changing.

And what made them change for me was discovering God's favourite colour.

As a boy I had imagined it was orange.
I knew that other boys my age believed it was green.

But now I know that it is neither of these colours; nor is it purple; nor is it red, white and blue.

God's favourite colour is ... tartan!

And that should be the colour of the Church ... tartan. Why? ... because nowhere in the Scripture does it suggest that we should all be the same, that we should be spiritual clones.

When Jesus sent out his disciples to preach the Gospel and establish the Church, he did not give them blueprints for how to organise worship, when or how often to have Holy Communion and whether or not to call it Mass, the Eucharist or the Lord's Supper.

So, from the beginning, there has been in the Church different practices, different expressions of faith and that, I believe, is in the purpose of God. We are not meant to be one colour, we are meant to be many. But, like tartan, we are only fulfilling our vocation to be the Church when one colour, one sector, one denomination does not predominate, but all complement each other.

I do not believe that Jesus wills the whole world to be Roman Catholic, Anglican, Baptist or Moravian.

I believe that Jesus wants the whole world to be Christian. And I believe that Jesus wants Christians to express their faith and their worship in different ways, yet to show unity by living alongside each other and relating to each other
> not as competitors but as co-operators,
> not as rivals but as co-workers,
> not as strangers but as friends.

Father Mitchell invited me, a Presbyterian minister, to preach to a completely Roman Catholic congregation.

I went not simply because Father Mitchell invited me, but also because I realised that in my life I had not just to take seriously the prayer of Jesus that all his followers should be one, but to use whatever opportunities came my way to express that unity visibly.

I hope that you, in your way,
may also take seriously the plea of Jesus to his Father;
and, as far as in you, become part of the answer to his prayer and never, please God,
never part of the problem.